BIGGEST NAMES IN SPORTS

JOSÉ ALTUVE

BASEBALL STAR

by Matt Tustison

FOCUS READERS

WWW.FOCUSREADERS.COM

Focus Readers is distributed by North Star Editions:
sales@northstareditions.com | 888-417-0195

Produced for Focus Readers by Red Line Editorial.

Photographs ©: Leslie Plaza Johnson/Icon Sportswire/AP Images, cover, 1; David J. Phillip/AP Images, 4–5; Eric Christian Smith/AP Images, 6; Kyodo/AP Images, 9; Ariana Cubillos/AP Images, 10–11; Alejandro Cegarra/AP Images, 12; Mike Janes/Four Seam Images/AP Images, 15; Pat Sullivan/AP Images, 16–17; Dave Einsel/AP Images, 18; John Rivera/Icon Sportswire/AP Images, 21; Cliff Welch/Icon Sportswire/AP Images, 22–23; Yi-Chin Lee/Houston Chronicle/AP Images, 25; Brett Coomer/Houston Chronicle/AP Images, 27; Red Line Editorial, 29

ISBN
978-1-63517-865-4 (hardcover)
978-1-63517-966-8 (paperback)
978-1-64185-169-5 (ebook pdf)
978-1-64185-068-1 (hosted ebook)

Library of Congress Control Number: 2018931323

Printed in the United States of America
Mankato, MN
May, 2018

ABOUT THE AUTHOR

Matt Tustison is a sports copy editor at the *Washington Post*. He also has worked as a sports copy editor at other newspapers, including the *Baltimore Sun*, and as an editor and writer of children's sports books.

TABLE OF CONTENTS

CHAPTER 1

WORLD SERIES CHAMPION

José Altuve wanted to start the 2017 **postseason** with a bang. The Houston Astros second baseman stepped up to the plate. It was his first at bat in Game 1 of the American League Division Series. Altuve took two strikes from Boston Red Sox pitcher Chris Sale. But on the third pitch, Altuve connected on a fastball.

Altuve watches the ball fly after swatting a home run.

Altuve celebrates one of his three home runs in Game 1 of the 2017 American League Division Series.

The ball sailed over the fence in center field. It was a home run!

Altuve didn't stop there. He hit two more homers in the game. That made

Altuve just the ninth player in history to hit three home runs in a postseason game.

Houston went on to defeat Boston in the series. The Astros' next opponent was the New York Yankees. Once again, Altuve was a star. He hit .320 with two more homers in the series. The Astros topped the Yankees in seven games to earn a trip to the World Series. Now they faced the Los Angeles Dodgers.

The Astros were shooting for their first title in team history. And Altuve was determined to make that happen. In Game 2, his home run in the 10th inning helped Houston win a thriller.

Game 5 was another classic. In the fifth inning, Altuve belted a three-run homer. Then, in the seventh inning, he hit a double that drove in a run. The Astros went on to win the game in 10 innings.

The World Series came down to Game 7. With two outs in the bottom

HOUSTON STRONG

In August 2017, Hurricane Harvey caused severe flooding in the Houston area. Thousands of people lost their homes. More than 75 people lost their lives. Houston was still recovering from the hurricane during the 2017 postseason. In honor of the city, every Astros player wore a patch that said "H Strong."

Altuve holds the championship trophy after the Astros' World Series victory.

of the ninth inning, the Astros were leading 5–1. The Dodgers' batter hit a grounder to second base. Altuve fielded the ball and threw it to the first baseman. The runner was out. The Astros were World Series champions!

CHAPTER 2

GROWING UP WITH BASEBALL

José Altuve was born on May 6, 1990. He grew up in Maracay, Venezuela. This South American city is passionate about baseball. Over the years, Maracay has been the starting point for more than 30 Major League Baseball (MLB) players.

José learned how to play baseball from his father, Carlos. José loved the game.

A baseball coach in Maracay helps young players practice.

Venezuelan players hone their skills at a field in Maracay.

He and his father played catch every day.

Sometimes they played without gloves.

As a child, José was a huge fan of major

league shortstop Omar Vizquel. Vizquel

also grew up in Venezuela. And at 5 feet 9 inches (175 cm), he was a short player just like José.

When José was 16, he took part in a two-day tryout that the Astros were holding in Maracay. He did not make the **cut** on the first day. The **scouts** thought José was too short and too small. After all, he stood only 5 feet 5 inches (165 cm) tall and weighed 140 pounds (64 kg).

But José's father encouraged him to return the next day. That's when José impressed several observers. The Astros offered José a minor league contract with a $15,000 signing bonus. He gladly accepted the deal.

The Astros put José in the Venezuelan Summer League in 2007. He excelled with a .343 batting average. José moved to the United States in 2008 so he could play for the Astros' minor league team in Greeneville, Tennessee. There he would continue to chase his dream of becoming a major league player.

LENDING A HELPING HAND

Off the field, Altuve has been involved with a number of charities to assist the less fortunate. In 2017, he started the José Altuve Foundation. The foundation raises money to support children with cancer. Altuve has also taken part in youth baseball clinics in both Houston and Maracay.

Altuve fields the ball during a minor league game in
2010.

CHAPTER 3

A DREAM COME TRUE

After two seasons with Greeneville, José Altuve was **promoted** to the next level of minor league baseball. Altuve's coaches saw a lot of potential in him. So in 2010, they moved him up another level. The small but talented second baseman was advancing quickly in the Astros' **farm system**.

Altuve gets a hit in his first major league game.

Altuve steals second base during a 2012 game against the Milwaukee Brewers.

In July 2011, Altuve's dream finally came true. The Astros called him up to the majors. Listed at 5 feet 6 inches

(168 cm), Altuve was one of the shortest players in Major League Baseball. But the 21-year-old quickly showed that he could compete in the big leagues. Altuve hit .276 for the Astros that year. However, despite his solid numbers, the Astros were terrible. They finished the season with the league's worst record.

In 2012, Altuve became one of baseball's top young stars. He was especially good at hitting and stealing bases. He also fielded well at second base. Altuve even made his first All-Star Game in 2012. But the Astros continued to struggle. Once again, they were the worst team in the league.

The next year, things got even worse for the Astros. They won only 51 games and lost 111. That was the worst record in team history. Even so, Altuve continued to play great. The team offered him a new contract that paid him millions of dollars. Altuve was quickly becoming the face of the **franchise**.

Altuve had an amazing year in 2014. He finished the season with a .341 batting average. That was the best average in the American League. Altuve also led the league with 225 hits and 56 stolen bases.

More importantly, the Astros were showing signs of improvement. They won 70 games and lost 92. The team

Altuve cranks out one of his many hits in 2014.

still wasn't good enough to reach the

postseason, but they were moving in the

right direction.

CHAPTER 4

ONE OF BASEBALL'S BEST

In 2015, José Altuve picked up right where he left off. The Astros star had a .313 batting average. And once again, he led the American League in stolen bases. Best of all, the Astros finally had a talented team. On the final day of the regular season, they **clinched** a spot in the Wild Card Game.

Altuve runs the bases after hitting the ball in a 2015 game.

It was the first time the Astros had reached the postseason in 10 years. Now they faced the New York Yankees in a one-game playoff. The winner would move on to the Division Series, and the loser would go home. In the seventh inning, the Astros were leading 2–0. That's when Altuve batted in a run to help his team seal the victory.

In the Division Series, the Astros lost to the Kansas City Royals. But Altuve had a lot to be proud of. He even won his first Gold Glove Award for his excellent defense.

Houston failed to reach the postseason in 2016. But Altuve was as good as ever.

Altuve shares a laugh with Aaron Judge, one of the tallest players in baseball.

He also showed more power than he had in previous seasons. He finished with a career-high 24 home runs.

In 2017, the Astros really blasted off. Altuve earned his third American League batting title. And the team got a major boost when they signed **veteran** pitcher Justin Verlander. The Astros finished with one of the best records in baseball. They went on to beat the Dodgers in a classic World Series.

A PURE HITTER

Altuve had a league-best 204 hits in 2017. That made him the first player in MLB history to lead his league in hits four years in a row. Altuve also became just the fifth player since the 1940s to have at least four straight seasons with 200 hits.

Thousands of fans attended the Astros' victory parade in Houston.

When the 2017 season was over, Altuve was named the American League Most Valuable Player. Altuve had shown that small players can accomplish big things.

JOSÉ ALTUVE

- Height: 5 feet 6 inches (168 cm)
- Weight: 165 pounds (75 kg)
- Birth date: May 6, 1990
- Birthplace: Maracay, Venezuela
- Minor league teams: Greeneville Astros (2008–09); Lancaster JetHawks (2010); Lexington Legends (2010); Corpus Christi Hooks (2011)
- MLB team: Houston Astros (2011–)
- Major awards: World Series champion (2017); American League Most Valuable Player (2017); Gold Glove Award (2015); American League batting champion (2014, 2016, 2017)

Lancaster

Lexington

Greeneville

Houston

Corpus Christi

Maracay

FOCUS ON
JOSÉ ALTUVE

Write your answers on a separate piece of paper.

1. Write a sentence that describes the main idea of Chapter 1.

2. Do you think Altuve is a better player because he is short? Why or why not?

3. Which team beat the Astros in the 2015 Division Series?

    A. Los Angeles Dodgers
    B. Kansas City Royals
    C. New York Yankees

4. Why didn't Altuve stay in the Astros' farm system for very long?

    A. The other players didn't want him on the team.
    B. He wanted to return to his home in Venezuela.
    C. He was good enough to move up to the major leagues.

Answer key on page 32.

GLOSSARY

clinched
Made certain that something would be won.

cut
When the number of players is reduced, leaving only the best players to continue.

farm system
A group of teams that help players develop their skills. Each MLB team has its own farm system. Good players usually move up to higher levels in the system.

franchise
A sports team.

postseason
A set of games played after the regular season to decide which team will be the champion.

promoted
Moved someone up to a higher level.

scouts
People whose jobs involve looking for talented young players.

veteran
A person who has been doing his or her job for a long time and has a lot of experience.

TO LEARN MORE

BOOKS

Aretha, David. *José Altuve: Champion Baseball Star*. New York: Enslow Publishing, 2018.

Fishman, Jon M. *José Altuve*. Minneapolis: Lerner Publications, 2018.

Roselius, J Chris. *Houston Astros*. Minneapolis: Abdo Publishing, 2015.

NOTE TO EDUCATORS

Visit **www.focusreaders.com** to find lesson plans, activities, links, and other resources related to this title.

INDEX

Answer Key: **1.** Answers will vary; **2.** Answers will vary; **3.** B; **4.** C